796.815

KICKBOXING BASICS

KT-427-143

Master Joe Fox & Art Michaels

Sterling Publishing Co., Inc.
New York

Loughborough College

LC032643

Disclaimer
As the author and the publisher have no control over how the reader chooses to utilize the information presented in this book and no capability of determining the reader's level of proficiency or physical condition, they are not responsible for injuries, mishaps, or other consequences that result from the reader's use of the information in this book.

LOU   ROUGH
C   E
L   RY

Library of Congress Cataloging-in-Publication Data

On file

Book Design by Judy Morgan
Edited by Rodman P. Neumann

3 5 7 9 10 8 6 4 2

Published by Sterling Publishing Company, Inc.
387 Park Avenue South, New York, N.Y. 10016
© 1998 by Master Joe Fox and Art Michaels
Distributed in Canada by Sterling Publishing
c/o Canadian Manda Group, One Atlantic Avenue, Suite 105
Toronto, Ontario, Canada M6K 3E7
Distributed in Great Britain and Europe by Cassell PLC
Wellington House, 125 Strand, London WC2R 0BB, England
Distributed in Australia by Capricorn Link (Australia) Pty Ltd.
P.O. Box 6651, Baulkham Hills, Business Centre, NSW 2153, Australia
Manufactured in the United States of America
All rights reserved

Sterling ISBN 0-8069-9781-8

With profound thanks and appreciation . . .

❏ To my wife, Cathy, my son, Sam, and my daughter, Jamie, for their patience and encouragement while I wrote and photographed this book.

❏ To my teacher and co-author, Master Joe Fox, who continues to teach me a wealth of martial arts.

❏ To Sensei Terry Nye and Sensei Karen Nye, Terry Nye's Kickboxing and Karate Gym, Lancaster, PA, for letting me take pictures in the gym, for patiently answering my questions, for informative interviews, and for reviewing some of the manuscript.

❏ To all the kickboxing students at Terry Nye's Kickboxing and Karate Gym for letting me interrupt their training and their classes to take pictures.

❏ To all the infinitely patient and cooperative kickboxers who let me take their pictures and who helped me behind the cameras and lights: Leah Mellinger, Jeramey McComsey, Douglas Esbenshade, Amy Clawson, Joe Goodman, Mark Mascari, Master Anthony Grafton, Janelle Silvers, Thelma Ramper, and Fred Waters.

❏ To Master Jim Harrison, Sakura Warrior Arts, Missoula, MT, for information in Chapter 7.

❏ To Vince "Black Tiger" Soberano, stuntman, retired kickboxing champion, and founder of the Black Tiger Muay Thai Gym, San Diego, CA, for chapters review and comment, and for photographs.

❏ To Larry Wilk, Boulder (CO) Karate, for chapters review and comment.

❏ To Allan Clarkin, Black Knights Kickboxing, Lancashire, England, for chapters review and comment.

❏ To Kyoshi John Therien and Sensei Brian Aylward, Therien Jiu-Jitsu and Kickboxing Dojo, Ottawa, Canada, for chapters review and comment.

❏ To Sherry and Ty Sterling, owners of Gold's Gym, Harrisburg, PA, for use of the facility to take photographs.

Art Michaels

Contents

Preface

Kickboxing training is hard work. You strive for maximums—alertness, conditioning, strength, and quickness. Kickboxing training is also a big challenge. The journey is difficult, but it's also exciting and rewarding. Every training session and every fight leads to greater insights into the sport and into yourself as a person and as an athlete.

Like other martial arts, kickboxing takes a long time to master. You get better at it only through effective training and coaching, continued practice of correct techniques, and experience in the ring.

Kickboxing is currently undergoing the kind of growth that boxing underwent some 60 or 70 years ago. Some professional boxers these days have as many as several hundred amateur fights before they enter the professional ranks. Some kickboxers, on the other hand, compete professionally after only a few fights.

That's not the fighters' fault; that's just the way this sport is evolving. Interest in kickboxing among men and

Train and fight hard, and enjoy the journey!

women is growing. Kickboxing's measure of skill at all levels is increasing because a growing number of fighters, men and women, have more amateur experience before they decide to fight professionally.

That's the purpose of this book. If you have some boxing experience, if you have some martial arts experience, and even if you have no experience in either of these areas, this book shows you the basics you need to learn step into the ring for your first amateur fight.

That fight could be one of several different kinds of kickboxing. As you train, you should focus your work on the kind of kickboxing you intend to pursue. This focus includes becoming thoroughly familiar with the rules under which you'll be fighting.

Generally speaking, there's full-contact karate, which features no kicking below the waist; another kind of kickboxing, similar to full-contact karate, allows leg kicks; and there's Muay Thai, or Thai boxing, in which punches and kicks are legal anywhere except to the groin, and where elbow and knee techniques, and some grabbing and holding techniques, are permitted. You will likely find fights that mix these rules. You'll also find "point kickboxing," which mixes punching and kicking with point-sparring rules.

For the most part, this book focuses on full-contact karate. See Chapter 7 for more information on the different kinds of kickboxing and how the training, strategy, and regulations differ among them.

No matter which kind of kickboxing you choose, you can-not learn the art from a book. You can, however, use this book as a supplement to your training in the basics of kickboxing, and as a reference as you train. This book offers an opportunity to learn a martial art that may otherwise not be available to you. It shows you how to find the coaches, trainers, promoters, training facilities and training partners you need, and it explains how to achieve the fitness and skill levels you need to get in the ring for your first amateur fight. This book also shows you how to win that fight!

The first order of business in achieving kickboxing skill is to attain a certain level of physical strength and stamina. That's how to start this worthy pursuit, at the beginning, and that starts with Chapter 1.

Train and fight hard, and enjoy the journey!

chapter one

STRENGTH TRAINING

As you learn the technical aspects of kickboxing, you need to develop your strength. Without strength, you cannot fight effectively. Strength training includes weight training that targets all the muscle groups. For punching, you need to develop the triceps, biceps, shoulder muscles, and latissimus muscles. For stability, it's important to condition the forearms and wrists. For kicking, develop the quadriceps, hamstrings, and calves. Developing the abdominals is important, too, for punching, kicking, and taking blows, and developing the lower back muscles supports the abdominals and leg muscles.

Focus first on developing power with heavy weights and a low number of repetitions. After you build the body to certain levels of strength in all the muscle groups, lessen the

More challenging abs work can be a product of your own ingenuity!

weight and increase the number of repetitions to increase stamina and speed.

Try to train conveniently, but be consistent. The best training arrangement is when all the required weights and equipment are in one place. If that's not the case, you have to spread out your training. For instance, on Monday, Wednesday, and Friday you train for strength in one gym. On Tuesday, Thursday, and Saturday, you train elsewhere for stamina.

The most effective training incorporates both machines and free weights. Free weights work well for strength training because you work more with a true weight. Machines are effective for stamina training because by their design they isolate muscles better than free weights. Machines are also safer to use for stamina training, because you perform a greater number of repetitions faster without the need for a spotter.

Consider the following specifics on how to build strength in all the muscle groups. These strength exercises are designed for high weights and low repetitions. How much weight to use initially depends on your current level of fitness. Choose a

Progressive work to build the abdominals includes crunches on an incline bench or incline chair. Hold weights across your chest to increase the challenge.

weight for each exercise that lets you perform eight to 10 repetitions in three sets. You should feel very tired and almost completely spent as you finish the third set. If you initially select too much weight, you may sacrifice form and limit your progress. You also increase the risk of injury. If you select too little weight, you focus more on stamina than on building strength.

Abdominals, Lower Back
. . . .

You summon kicking and punching power from the lower abdominal area, which is supported by the lower back muscles, so developing the abs and

lower back is essential. Work the abs with several kinds of crunches, raises, lifts, and machine work.

Work the lower abdominal muscles in another kind of crunch by drawing the knees and shoulders together.

Work leg lifts for more advanced strengthening of the abs.

First, with no weights, lie flat, bend your knees, and place your arms across your chest. For one kind of crunch, just lift the shoulders. Work the lower abdominal muscles in another kind of crunch by drawing the knees and shoulders together. Place weights on your chest in both exercises to create more resistance. Use a crunch machine, incline chair, or incline bench for advanced strengthening of the abs.

Exercise the lower back muscles with raises in an apparatus for this purpose. Standing with the legs about a shoulder-width apart, bend the knees slightly and pull the weight up.

Legs

Kicking effectively calls for strengthening the quadriceps, hamstrings, and calves, as well as the inner thigh muscles and hip flexors. First, exercise the quadriceps with leg extensions. Then work the hamstrings with leg curls.

In a standing calf, you push weights up with pads on your shoulders.

Three exercises are effective for strengthening the calves—standing calves, donkey calves, and seated calves. In a standing calf, you push weights up with pads on your shoulders. In a donkey calf,

exercise the lower back muscles with weight raises.

you stand bent over and push up weights on your back. In a seated calf, you push up weights on your knees from a seated position.

The quadriceps lift the legs. Conditioned calves and quads help you jump quickly and high, and conditioned hamstrings help you perform powerful front kicks, side kicks, ax kicks, and hook kicks.

exercise the quadriceps with leg extensions.

In a seated calf, you push up weights on your knees from a seated position.

Strong calves also help you execute fast, powerful blitzes and takeoffs.

A program on a cable crossover machine can help you develop the inner thigh and hip flexor muscles, as can work on other machines designed to isolate these muscles.

Work the hamstrings with leg curls.

Forearms

Wrist curls and squeezing a tennis ball can help you develop the forearms, wrists, and hand muscles. Developing these muscles is necessary to support your fists and for blocking effectively.

The pulling, gripping, and pushing you perform in other weight room exercises works your forearms, wrists, and

Squeezing a tennis ball can help develop the forearms, wrists, and hand muscles.

Wrist curls can also help you develop the forearms, wrists, and hand muscles. Developing these muscles is necessary to support your fists and for blocking effectively.

hands, but further isolating these parts increases your strength and endurance.

To perform one kind of wrist curl, while seated hold a dumbbell in one hand and support your arm on your leg. Hold the hand either palm-up or palm-down. Curl the bar through your wrist's full range of motion for one repetition. You can perform this exercise with barbells, too.

Perform another effective wrist curl first by winding a rope around a dowel or bar and tying a weight to the end. As you turn the bar with the hands and wrists—curling the rope up and down—move the bar up and down with the wrists. Add more weight as your strength increases.

to perform the military press, lift the barbell or dumbbells up and behind the neck. The military press exercises the trapezius muscle and the back part of the shoulder.

Work the front part of the shoulder in front raises with dumbbells.

Shoulders, Biceps, Triceps

Punching and blocking require strong shoulder muscles. Developing each part of the shoulder muscles is important. Four lifts cover the entire shoulder muscles—military press, front raise, side raise, and bent-over raise.

To perform the military press, lift the barbell or dumbbells up and behind the neck. The military press exercises

exercise the sides of the shoulders with side raises.

the trapezius muscle and the back part of the shoulder. Work the front part of the shoulder in front raises with dumbbells. Exercise the sides of the shoulders with side raises, and work the back part of the shoulder and the traps again with bent-over raises.

Work the back part of the shoulder and the trapezius muscle with bent-over raises.

Exercise the biceps in two or three lifts. Kickboxing does not require the biceps to be as developed as other muscle groups. But strong biceps help in pulling and in the general conditioning of the arms. That's important for blocking and for keeping the guard up even when the arms are fatigued.

exercise the biceps with standing curls using either dumbbells or a barbell.

Exercise the biceps first with standing or seated curls, using either dumbbells or a barbell. Then perform concentrated curls. To perform a concentrated curl, place the elbow on the knee while seated. This isolates the biceps more than standing or seated curls. Placing the arm on an inclined support is another way to perform concentrated curls. A preacher curl isolates the biceps the most. In a preacher curl you place the upper arms over a pad while seated. Per-

forming other curls, you "cheat" a little by letting other muscles help you perform the curl. "Cheating" is most difficult with a preacher curl, because this exercise isolates the muscle directly.

Conditioned triceps and shoulder muscles are important for punching power, even though the triceps and shoulder muscles are two of the least used muscles in everyday activity. Begin working the tri-

to perform a concentrated curl, place the elbow on the knee while seated. This isolates the biceps more than standing or seated curls. Placing the arm on an inclined support is another way to perform concentrated curls.

ceps with push-downs—grasping a bar positioned close to the body and pushing straight down.

You should also perform triceps extensions with a machine or with a barbell. In this exercise, you sit in an inclined position and push the weight upward. A third triceps exercise is a kickback. Position the arm at about 90-degrees and push a weight backward, twisting the arm.

a preacher curl isolates the biceps the most. Place the upper arms over a pad while seated.

Work the triceps with push-downs. Grasp a bar positioned close to the body and push straight down.

You should also perform triceps extensions with a machine or with a barbell. Sit in an inclined position or stand and push the weight upward.

to isolate the inner chest muscles, perform flies or use a pec (pectoral) deck machine.

a conditioning program for the back muscles begins with front and back lat pulldowns. Front pulldowns isolate the middle and lower lats.

back pulldowns work the upper lats.

begin the chest exercises by working the upper chest muscles with bench presses using barbells.

Chest, Back Muscles

A conditioning program for the back muscles begins with front and back lat pulldowns. Front pulldowns isolate the middle and lower lats. Back pulldowns work the upper lats.

You should also perform low rows, which exercise the middle and upper lats, and dumbbell rows, which work all the upper back muscles.

Punching and blocking most often use the upper and inner chest muscles, so isolating these muscles is important. Work the chest muscles with three exercises.

Begin the chest exercises working the upper chest muscles with bench presses using barbells. To isolate the inner chest muscles, perform flies or use a pec (pectoral) deck machine. Work the upper and front chest muscles with a dip machine.

Work the upper and front chest muscles with a dip apparatus.

Work It to Failure

The goal of these strength-building exercises is to work the muscles to failure. This means that when you near the end of each exercise's third set, you simply can't move the weight. The theory in exercising a muscle to failure this way is that you fatigue the muscle completely so that when you rest, the muscle rebuilds stronger.

"Exercising muscles to failure" and "challenging muscles" are different strategies with different results. Challenging tones and firms a weakened or injured muscle, and it's used to build stamina and speed, but exercising a muscle to failure breaks the muscle down. When you rest, the muscle renews itself stronger. You can increase your strength a little by working out until you tire, but you won't gain as much strength as you would when you exercise the muscle to failure.

As you perform all of these lifts, remember to move through your full range of motion. Maintaining good form lets each muscle benefit the most from each set of repetitions. If you cannot maintain good form throughout each lift's sets, lower the weight or decrease the number of repetitions in each of your sets.

STRETCHING TO INCREASE FLEXIBILITY

Increasing flexibility is a product of increasing muscle strength. Increasing flexibility for kickboxing most often requires strengthening the leg muscles that support the hip joints, and stretching. In this case, "flexibility" for kicking involves the range of motion in the hip joints.

A few times each week, before your cooldown stretching, work on stretching the lower back muscles, inner thigh muscles, buttocks muscles (hip flexors), quadriceps, and hamstrings to increase your flexibility. This kind of stretching requires you to hold stretches a little longer than you would for warm-up and cooldown stretching. You should also try to stretch a bit farther than you do for warm-up and cooldown. The goal is to feel just a bit more than mild discomfort. But the same rules apply in stretching to increase flexibility as in warm-up and cooldown stretching: Sharp, piercing pain or burning pain means you're overstretching.

After this stretching, perform your usual cooldown work. It's important to stretch to increase flexibility after the strenuous part of a workout. The legs are tired then and fully warm; also, exhausted muscles are less likely to resist your efforts to stretch a bit farther.

Why increase flexibility? The more range of motion a joint has, the more speed it can generate when delivering a kick. Speed is the main ingredient in power. Thus, as the range of motion in a joint increases, so do its speed and power.

Stretching to increase flexibility requires you to hold stretches a little longer than you would for warm-up and cooldown stretching. You should also try to stretch a bit farther than you do for warm-up and cooldown. It's important to stretch to increase flexibility after the strenuous part of a workout. The legs are tired then and fully warm, and exhausted muscles are less likely to resist your efforts to stretch a bit farther.

Stretching regularly before and after each weight-room workout and incorporating your full range of motion in all these lifts and exercises can help you increase your flexibility as you increase your strength.

When to Exercise

When you exercise to increase strength, don't work the same muscle group on two consecutive days. Remember that rest is very important when you take muscles to failure. If you don't let the muscles rest so that they can rebuild, you risk injury, and your progress will surely be slowed. Don't work the whole body every day, either. You should be fatigued after you work one major muscle group. Trying to extend the workout to bring another muscle group to failure when you're already tired means, again, you increase the risk of injury and you won't get the best results.

The best strategy is to work one muscle group each day, or exercise two different muscle groups per workout. For instance, in one session, work the chest and triceps. Then in the next session exercise the biceps and back; in the next

session, the shoulders and legs. The key to creating the most effective strength-building weight training program is to let the muscles rest at least one day after taking them to failure.

Warm-up and Cooldown Stretching

Readying the muscles for more vigorous exercise by increasing the blood flow to the muscles is the purpose of warm-up stretching. Cooldown stretching helps tensed muscles "remember" to stay long and stretched. Stretching also aids circulation, helping the muscle cells take in more nutrients and carry away waste more efficiently.

Warm-up and cooldown stretching is gentle. It is not meant to increase flexibility. In warm-up and cooldown stretching you should feel a slight discomfort in the muscles. Experiencing burning pain or piercing, sharp pain means you're stretching too hard and you should ease off the stretch a little.

If you stretch with a partner, be sure your communication signals are clear so that your partner doesn't injure you

Warm up before you stretch. Generally speaking, this means exercising lightly until you begin to sweat. Warm-up and cooldown exercises include calisthenics like jumping jacks, jumping rope, jogging, shadow boxing, and similar activities.

inadvertently by holding a stretch longer than you want. When you're helping your partner stretch, don't "pull" or "push." Think of this kind of help as simply adding weight.

Warm up before you stretch. Generally speaking, this means exercising lightly until you begin to sweat. Warm-up and cooldown exercises include calisthenics like jumping jacks, jumping rope, jogging, shadow boxing, and similar activities.

For both your warm-up and cooldown, stretch the muscles twice with a minute or so between stretches. Let each stretch last 30 seconds to about a minute or two.

Breathing Patterns and Lifting

Don't hold your breath when you begin a set of lifts and exhale at the end of the set, or when you cannot hold the air in any longer. As you begin a lift, exhale through the mouth.

When you begin to return the weight to the starting position, inhale through your nose. Breathe rhythmically this way as you lift.

Breathing correctly during weight-room workouts lets you get the most from each repetition and set. Holding your breath, or otherwise breathing

Readying the muscles for more vigorous exercise by increasing the blood flow to them is the purpose of warm-up stretching. Cooldown stretching helps tensed muscles "remember" to stay long and stretched. Warm-up and cooldown stretching are gentle. In warm-up and cooldown stretching, you should feel a slight discomfort in the muscles. Experiencing burning pain or piercing, sharp pain means you're stretching too hard and should ease off the stretch a little. If you stretch with a partner, be sure your communication signals are clear, so that your partner doesn't injure you inadvertently by holding a stretch longer than you want.

incorrectly during lifting, limits the oxygen delivered to the muscles. Breathing correctly brings the most oxygen to the muscles. Limiting the muscle's oxygen supply means that the muscle will produce lactic acid quickly. The "burning" you feel in a taxed muscle indicates that the muscle is producing lactic acid. Lactic acid production signals that the muscle's oxygen requirement isn't being met and that the muscle can no longer meet the demand. Correct breathing brings the most oxygen to the muscle, so that it doesn't fatigue as quickly as it would with an inadequate oxygen supply. (See Chapter 2 on stamina training for more specifics on how to establish a beneficial breathing pattern.)

chapter two

STAMINA TRAINING

Stamina training means building two kinds of stamina—muscle stamina, increased primarily with weight training and kicking and punching drills, and breathing stamina.

Breathing stamina is important because it develops you aerobically to fight in two- or three-minute rounds and recover within a minute. You can develop strong kicking and punching techniques and superb technical abilities, but if you cannot recover for the next round within one minute, you'll last only one round. You'll be tired in the legs and arms, and you won't be mentally as sharp. That's when a fighter with lesser technical ability can beat a more proficient, better fighter.

Running and Controlling the Breathing

Running is a large part of stamina training. Your goal is to train for a three- to six-round fight. You should build your stamina first by running five miles with times of five to six minutes per mile.

During this distance run, get into the habit of controlling the breathing. Controlled breathing helps you fatigue less, and you bring in the maximum amount

gains in conditioning come the slowest. Persistence is the key.

of oxygen to delay as long as possible the production of lactic acid in the muscles. The muscles produce lactic acid when they use up the available oxygen supply. Production of lactic acid is the "burning" you feel in a muscle when you ask it to go beyond its endurance limit.

To control the breathing, establish a breathing pattern. First, inhale deeply and slowly through your nose for a few seconds. Hold the air in for several seconds. Then slowly exhale through the mouth with the mouth open slightly. This holds the oxygen longer in the lungs, letting the oxygen diffuse more thoroughly into the bloodstream. The more oxygen reserve you have, the longer you can run, train, and fight without tiring.

How does the body become more efficient with this kind of breathing? The idea is that inhaling through the nose causes the diaphragm to bring oxygen into the lower portion of the lungs. The lower portion of the lungs has more capacity to exchange nutrients than the middle and upper portions. Inhaling through the mouth brings air mostly into the upper and middle portions of the lungs. Thus, muscle cells can exchange nutrients and

Running is a large part of stamina training. Your goal is to train for a three- to six-round fight. Build your stamina first by running five miles with times of five to six minutes per mile.

waste more efficiently when air reaches the lower portions of the lungs.

However, when you're running and training, and getting tired, controlling the breathing isn't easy. Nor does it feel comfortable at first. The natural response to tiring is rapid, shallow breathing. When you pant this way you require a long time to recover, because you take in only a little oxygen, mostly into the upper and middle portions of the lungs. Then it's exhaled rapidly before the oxygen has time to diffuse into the lungs and bloodstream.

Most kickboxing students know that controlling the breathing is important, but they don't realize that it takes a lot of training to be comfortable with controlling the breathing. Distance running helps you develop the breathing pattern as a habit, so that you don't have to think about it. At first, controlling the breathing makes you believe you're out of breath, as if you have to gasp for air. But learning to breathe correctly lets you shorten your recovery time and last much longer than you would otherwise. Progress might seem slowest in this area, but stick with it because the benefits are unquestionably worth it.

At a more advanced level, controlling the breathing lets you hide your fatigue from an opponent—no matter how tired you might actually be, all the opponent sees is your controlled breathing. The opponent will not see the usual signs of tiring—panting with the mouth open.

most kickboxing students already know that controlling the breathing is important, but they may not realize that it takes a lot of training to be comfortable with controlling the breathing. Distance running helps you develop the breathing pattern as a habit, so that you don't have to think about it.

Wind Sprints

After running the long distance, perform wind sprints. On a soccer field or football field, mark off 50 yards. You sprint the 50 yards all out, and then walk back to the starting point, which takes about a minute. As soon as you reach the starting point, turn around and take off again for another 50-yard all-out sprint.

During your walk back to the starting point, concentrate on breathing exercises and recovery time. This walk-back time simulates the one-minute recovery time you have between rounds.

Start with about 10 cycles of wind sprints, and build the cycle to 20 repetitions. The 20th cycle isn't going to be as fast as the first few, but on that 20th cycle you can still perform all out and give it some burst of speed and strength.

You might also try a different kind of wind sprint. Pick a starting point and sprint as fast as you can, arms pumping. As soon as you feel yourself starting to slow, stop and walk. When you regain your wind, do it again. Try to make your sprints longer as you train. Even if you manage only 20 feet before you notice your-

after running the long distance, perform wind sprints. Sprint 50 yards all out, and then walk back to the starting point, which takes about a minute. As soon as you reach the starting point, turn around and take off again for another 50-yard all-out sprint. This walk-back time simulates the one-minute recovery time you have between rounds.

self tiring, continue with this training. The idea is to lengthen the sprint period.

No matter which wind sprint method you decide to try, remember that people have different starting points, depending on what they've been doing before kickboxing training. Those already in good condition can start with more cycles and with a longer period, before they notice they're tiring; those less physically fit can start with fewer cycles and shorter distances. Wind-sprint training is a prerequisite to going into the ring. In the ring you continue to build your stamina, but you add the technical parts of fighting.

Recovery Time Is the Key

Make no mistake about it: Gains in stamina are the slowest and most difficult to make and measure. When you want to test your progress, don't see how quickly you tire, because if you're not getting tired, you're not pushing hard enough. The best measure of progress is seeing your recovery time become shorter and shorter. The faster you can recover, the better condition you're in.

Sometimes amateur fighters aren't evenly matched. The technically better fighter might not be in as good a condition as the opponent. If the less technically proficient fighter can make it through the first or second round, his conditioning will help him beat a technically superior opponent.

Muscle Stamina

Muscle stamina comes through repetitious strength training with weights, bag work, kicking, and punching. Use the same exercises for increasing muscle stamina as you do for increasing muscle strength. However, for stamina training, lower the weight and increase the number of repetitions. Perform the reps faster than you would for building strength.

To work the arms and shoulders a bit differently, for instance, shadow box while holding five-pound dumbbells. Or when you perform bag work, use the jab. You're working the muscles for stamina with all these routines. At first, when you perform these exercises, your arm feels like lead. After a while, your jab becomes faster and stronger because your conditioning—

muscle stamina—improves. You can pop the jab faster, and you're neither tired during the workout nor sore later.

Kicking and punching drills with a heavy bag and focus pads are also effective builders of muscle stamina. The key is repetitive work. Once you

develop technically and your conditioning gives you a certain amount of staying power, begin exercising in complete rounds with bag work. To develop the ability to fight through two-minute rounds, work six minutes with a one-minute rest between rounds.

muscle stamina comes through repetitious strength training with weights, bag work, kicking, and punching. When working with a bag, try just jabs or one or two kinds of kicks at first. Later you'll really "mix it up" with combinations of punching and kicking in your stamina workout on the bag.

Work three times as long as you would in a fight, because getting hit and taking blows is much more tiring: A two-minute round facing an opponent will seem like six minutes of solo bag work.

This conditioning comes slowly, in steps. About a month before your first fight, work mostly in the ring to bring all your technique and conditioning to a peak. You want to establish this peak just before you fight.

To work the arms and shoulders for stamina a bit differently, shadow box while holding five-pound dumbbells.

Kicking and punching drills with focus pads are also effective builders of muscle stamina. The key is repetitive work.

Conditioning to Take a Blow

If you're easily winded by a body punch or kick, that is, if you can't breathe when you're hit, you can't fight or defend yourself. For this reason, conditioning the body is important. Practicing different drills with a medicine ball is useful. Work with a medicine ball simulates a blow to the body. Passing the ball and letting it hit your stomach is one exercise. When you pass the ball, let it strike the middle abdominal muscles

In this medicine ball exercise, you lie on the training room floor while your partner drops the medicine ball onto your abdomen. With each strike, tense the abs and exhale.

Work with a medicine ball simulates a blow to the body and helps condition the abdominal area. Passing the ball and letting it hit your stomach is one exercise. When you pass the ball, let it strike the middle abdominal muscles and obliques. The drill also works all the arm muscles.

and obliques. The drill also works all the arm muscles.

In circular training, twist the torso to pass the ball to a partner behind you, and, twisting the other way, slam the ball into your stomach on the way back. You can also pass the ball back and forth without catching it—you let the ball hit your stomach and "catch" it in your body.

In another exercise with a medicine ball, you and a partner face each other and throw the ball at each other's midsections. While you're practicing this exercise, learn how to move so that you don't take the full force of the strike.

In yet another medicine ball exercise, you lie on the training-room floor while your partner drops the medicine ball onto your abdomen. With each strike, tense the abs and exhale. You can also toss the medicine ball in the air yourself in this exercise. Tossing the ball by yourself also lets you work the triceps, shoulders, and chest muscles.

Sit-ups and conditioning work on an ab machine are also good training in learning how to take a blow. The better your muscles are conditioned, the less they'll just "sink in" when you're hit. When you're out of condition, the muscles "sink in" when you're hit, and a blow could damage your internal organs. For this reason, appropriate abdominal training is important. The more the abs are developed, the more power you can draw from the lower abdomen and the more effective your offensive techniques and defense will be.

In one such kickboxing class exercise, the men line up opposite the women. The women then punch the men in the abdomen. The women drill their punching combinations; the men condition the abs to take a blow. One trainer calls this drill "spot reducing."

tossing the medicine ball by yourself also lets you work the triceps, shoulders, and chest muscles.

In one kickboxing class exercise, the men line up opposite the women. The women then punch the men in the abdomen. The women drill their punching combinations; the men condition the abs to take a blow.

chapter three

BOXING SKILLS

For most of your initial amateur fights, you'll use more boxing skills than kicking skills. Kicking is set up by a lot of boxing techniques. For these reasons, developing refined boxing skills is important if you aspire to go anywhere with your kickboxing.

Jab

If you're just starting, work on basic punching and blocking skills with the hands. The first punch to learn is the jab. The jab is important because it's used to set up other techniques and feel out an opponent—assess the opponent's strengths and weaknesses. It also is used defensively to end a combination and thwart an opponent's counterattack. Jabbing also lets you develop a feeling for distance with your opponent. The jab is used to attack the opponent's chin, nose, and eyes. The weapon is the knuckles of the index and middle fingers. This weapon is the same for all these punches.

The jab isn't particularly powerful. The lead hand snaps out and back with the same kind of twisting motion as a right cross. The better boxers are those with excellent jabs—they keep a jabbing fist in the opponent's face (and a kickboxer keeps a jabbing front leg in the opponent's body). This often confuses an opponent and lets you set up other combinations. Furthermore, the corkscrew motion of executing a jab can tear the opponent's skin.

However, in kickboxing, you use the hand jab about half the time or less, using the lead-leg front kick most often as a jab. Using both jabs is effective. Using primarily a hand jab, though, sooner or later a good kicker will catch you squarely in the ribs.

Developing an effective jab requires a lot of drilling. If you've ever tried to jab for two minutes, you know how fatiguing it is on the shoulder. If you're not trained properly, after one round a jab can become ineffective. If the arm isn't conditioned properly, once the arm fatigues the guard drops and leaves you vulnerable to your opponent's most powerful techniques, those coming directly from the front. A fatigued arm is also slow to rise to block a kick or punch coming straight at you.

As you increase your stamina, you should punch and jab holding five-pound dumbbells. After this kind of workout, jabbing without the weights will seem effortless.

Ending a combination with a jab lets you create distance from your opponent and momentarily retreat safely.

the jab is important because it is used to set up other techniques and feel out an opponent. Start in a fighting position with the left leg forward.

One kind of jab is meant to be used by itself. It's a probing technique, a distancing tool, and a defensive move. Throw the jab, twisting the fist as you hit the target. At the same time, though, move the head and upper torso to the right (arrow). This keeps your head a moving target, and makes your opponent miss if he jabs at the same time.

the second kind of jab is used when you jab in combination with a right cross or other punch. In this case, you would not move the head. It's important to practice both kinds of jabs.

To start, learn to execute two kinds of jabs. The first jab is meant to be used by itself. It's a probing technique, a distancing tool, and a defensive move. From a fighting position, throw the jab, twisting the fist as you hit the target. At the same time, though, as you jab with the forward left hand, for instance, move the head to the right. This keeps your head a moving target, and makes your opponent miss if he jabs at the same time.

The second kind of jab is used when you jab in combination with a right cross or other punch. In this case, you would not move the head.

It's important to practice both kinds of jabs.

Right Cross

Once a person has an effective jab, it's wise to work on a straight, up-the-middle right cross. A right cross, also

Once a person has an effective jab, it's wise to work on a straight, up-the-middle right cross. A right cross, also called a straight right or a reverse punch, is a straight line to the opponent and the quickest way to reach him. Start in a fighting stance with the left foot forward.

After throwing a left jab, this powerful punch incorporates turning the shoulders and hips, and twisting the fist at the point of execution to add a measure of additional power and focus. Work this punch so that you get your hip, shoulder and more of the body into the punch. In this way your right cross is much more powerful than just punching with the arm. The right cross's power comes from pivoting on the ball of the rear foot (arrow). In this way you don't change position to throw the punch or open yourself for counter, and the pivot gives you much more reach without putting your face closer to the opponent.

called a straight right or a reverse punch, is a straight line to the opponent and the quickest way to reach him. The right cross is a knockout strike that by its power and speed should at least command your opponent's respect.

This powerful punch incorporates turning the shoulders and hips, and twisting the fist at the point of execution to add a measure of additional power and focus. You begin a simple combination with a jab, and then follow it immediately with a right cross. You work this punch so that you get your hip, shoulder and more of the body into the punch. In this way your right cross is much more powerful than simply punching with the arm. The right cross's power comes from pivoting on

an uppercut is effective for targeting the chin, but you can also effectively hit the floating ribs and solar plexus. Turning the shoulders and hips into your uppercuts makes them more powerful. Start in a fighting position with the left foot forward.

bend slightly to the right, practicing dodging an opponent's left jab.

Come back powerfully with the uppercut, striking the opponent's chin from underneath his left jab. Remember to follow through on this punch.

the ball of the rear foot. In this way you don't change position to throw the punch or open yourself for counter, and the pivot gives you much more reach without putting your face closer to the opponent.

Uppercut

This powerful strike is effective for targeting the chin, but you can also effectively hit the floating ribs and solar plexus.

Turning the shoulders and hips into your uppercuts makes them more powerful. An uppercut can be used as a single punch in some circumstances, but for the most part, learn to set up an uppercut as part of combinations.

Hook Punch

A hook can be executed with either hand in a fighting stance, but from the back

hand—right hand, in this example—a hook is more powerful because you can put more of the body into the punch. You twist the body and shoulders to perform a hook punch with either hand, but direct the hips and shoulders inward, not straight ahead as you would with a right cross. The hook punch is effective for targeting the opponent's head and body.

Before you learn the hook punch, it's best to become proficient and effective with a jab

a hook punch can be executed with either hand in a fighting stance, but from the back hand—right hand in this example—a hook is more powerful because you can put more of the body into the punch. Start in a fighting stance with the left foot forward.

twist the body and shoulders to the left to perform a right hook. Direct the hips and shoulders inward, not straight ahead as you would with a right cross. The elbow follows the path of the fist.

35

a spinning backfist can be remarkably effective. Start in a fighting stance with the left leg forward. Set it up with jabs and straight rights so that the opponent's hands are in front of his face.

Spin clockwise, turning the head and torso so that you can see the target. As you turn, cock the arm at the elbow.

extend the right hand so that its whipping motion meets the target as you come around in the spin. The torque you generate in spinning increases this technique's power. You want to strike the target as you come around—not before or after you complete the spin. The target is the opponent's side of the face, unguarded momentarily while the opponent has his hands directly in front of his face.

and a right cross. If you work a lot of hooks at the beginning, while you're learning straight punches, you may tend to hook your straight punches. This lessens the driving power of clean, straight shots like the jab and right cross. Remember that in hook punches, the elbow follows the path of the fist. In straight punches, keep the elbows close to the body so that the punch stays on a straight-line path.

As you practice hooks, get into the habit of keeping the fist upright—don't punch with the palm down. Your hook punches will be stronger this way, because you're more likely to hit the opponent with the knuckles of the index and middle fingers—the weapon. Performing hook punches with the palm down, placing the pinkie and ring finger knuckles closest to the opponent, could weaken this punch and increase the risk of injury to those fingers.

The reason why the weapon in all these punches is the knuckles of the index and middle fingers is that the bones of the arm support these two fingers more than they support the ring finger and pinkie.

As you learn strategy and gain ring experience, you'll see that a hook punch with the forward hand works best with a fast opponent. Hooks with the rear hand work best when the opponent is a brawler.

You might also try a double hook. This punch combination can be effective when it's set up. You start with a straight right so that the opponent places his hands in front of his face to block. Then you come again quickly with a right hook to the side of the face, and double up on that punch, throwing it twice quickly.

Spinning Backfist

A spinning backfist can be remarkably effective. From a fighting stance with the left leg forward, begin spinning clockwise, turning the head and torso so that you can see the target. As you turn, cock the arm at the elbow and extend the right hand so that its whipping motion meets the target as you come around in the spin. The torque you generate in spinning increases this technique's power. You want to strike the target as you come around—not before or after you complete the spin. The target is the opponent's jaw or side of the face. Practice following through

with the right hand—don't just stop the hand motion as you hit the target.

As you practice the spinning backfist, get into the habit of keeping the left hand up in a guarding position to protect your left side from counterattack, and work in a defensive jab, kick, or other following technique as a combination with this punch.

Stances, Foot Position, Hand Position

When you practice punching, get in the habit of remaining in a good stance. Keep both fists up about cheek-high, and keep the elbows and forearms in so that you protect your ribs and offer only the narrowest path to the chest. In this position it's easier to deflect a strike to the center part of the body.

If you have a martial-arts background, you might be comfortable with a more "sideways" stance, so that the body isn't squared off to the opponent. For kickboxing, though, you want to square off the body a bit more. In a more traditional martial-arts side stance, the only punch you can execute effectively is the jab, and it's difficult to perform a powerful rear kick or right cross without greatly telegraphing the movement. So in kickboxing, fight more from a squared-off position—not squared off straight onto the opponent, but just a little more squared off than in a traditional martial-arts stance.

Position the legs so that they are about a shoulder-width apart. You carry this over into kickboxing from other martial arts because you have a lower center of gravity and it's easy to move from one side to another and forward and backward. This position is very stable, and you have complete control over the legs and arms. If your stance is too narrow, you might be off balance when you get hit. If your feet are nearly together, the stance is unstable. If the feet are too far apart, moving and executing kicks become difficult. Then you have to bring the feet a little closer together to throw a kick, and that slows the technique and telegraphs it to the opponent.

Bobbing and Weaving

Watch the better boxers. Their bobbing and weaving makes them elusive targets. When you move the body a lot, you become a moving target, and that's harder to hit cleanly than a stationary one. Moving the head is important, too, because even if an opponent has good body movement, the head stays relatively stationary. You anticipate where the

●ne effective drill for learning the bobbing and weaving movement involves tying a rope to the top ring rope and stretching it straight out across the center of the ring. You dip, come up, and step as you walk up the rope. Practice dipping down from the torso and knees instead of leaning forward with the head to dip.

dip under the rope, keeping the guard up

Come up on the other side of the rope

dip under the rope again

Come up on the other side of the rope

When you can perform this drill effectively, as you come up and step, add a punching combination—such as a jab or an uppercut. The dipping and rising add driving power to the punching techniques. Always keep your head up, looking at your opponent.

target will be after you watch an opponent for a few rounds. If the head stays stationary, sooner or later an alert fighter will find a good, clean shot to that target.

It's important to understand that bobbing and weaving for kickboxers is a little different than it is for boxers. Never duck too low, as a boxer might. If you duck too low, you might lean right into an opponent's knee as he starts to kick. This is a problem most often associated with boxers who become kickboxers.

One effective walking drill for learning the bobbing and weaving movement involves tying a rope to the top ring rope and stretching it straight out across the center of the ring. You dip, come up, and step as you walk up the rope. Practice dipping down from the torso and knees instead of leaning forward with the head to dip.

When you can perform this drill effectively, as you come up and step, add a punching combination—such as a jab or an uppercut. The dipping and rising add driving power to the

another drill for learning to bob and weave is to have a partner put on focus pads and throw punches toward your head. Your partner isn't trying to hit you in this case. The idea is that you bob and weave to make your partner miss. You also learn to keep moving, as you punch, punch, bob; punch, punch, bob. You can work endless kinds of combinations with this drill. Start with a jab.

punching techniques. Always keep your head up, looking at your opponent.

Another drill for learning to bob and weave is to have a partner put on focus pads and throw punches toward your head. Your partner isn't trying to hit you in this case. The idea is that you bob and weave to make your partner miss. You also learn to keep moving, as you punch, punch, bob; punch, punch, bob.

Fighting this way and controlling the body are difficult skills to learn. To be effective, moving and controlling the body requires a lot of work. Even for someone who moves well in the ring, this motion is unnatural and requires much practice.

Continue with a right cross

duck under the opponent's left jab

Come up with a right cross

chapter four

KICKING SKILLS

n most amateur kickboxing fights, competitors must throw a minimum number of kicks, usually four or six. A kick judge counts the number of kicks competitors perform. This judge counts only kicks that he believes could hurt the opponent—he doesn't count kicks that are executed half-heartedly. In a two- or three-minute round, four or six strong kicks is a lot. It takes much more energy to throw an effective kick than it does to punch, so developing strong, effective kicks with powerful punches lets you balance your arsenal.

The basic, main kicking weapons for kickboxing are the front kick, football kick, round-house kick, side kick, hook kick, and ax kick. The front-leg sweep isn't considered a "kick," even though it really is. It's important also to learn how to execute this technique

and defend against it. These kicks are used most often because they are the most effective. Spinning and jump-spinning kicks are more advanced techniques.

Don't be fooled into thinking that an arsenal only of basic kicks is ineffective and that you need flashy jumping and

jump-spinning kicks to win. You will eventually combine all these basic kicks into many, many combinations. You'll practice so that you mix these kicks with punches and other techniques. The idea is to become fluid, creative, and unpredictable. Developing a foundation with basic kicking

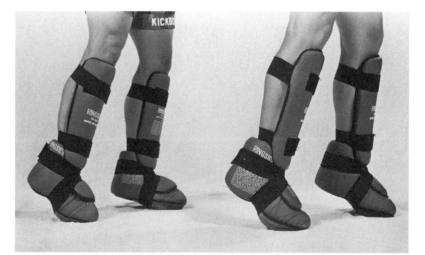

If you're new to kicking, train and condition the muscles around the toes to bend the toes back and expose the ball-of-the-foot weapon. One way to accomplish this is to walk around the training area every day for a few minutes on the balls of your feet.

42

and punching techniques is important because fighters who use only what comes naturally are one-dimensional, and they can be beaten by more versatile opponents. Building a firm foundation in kicking and punching helps you expand your offensive and defensive repertoire and gives you the edge when you must adapt to each opponent's varied strengths and weaknesses.

Study tapes and videos of kickboxing matches carefully. The fact is, champions do know the fancy, advanced techniques, but they win most matches with basic kicking and punching skills.

Front Kick

To perform a front kick, in a ready position with the left leg forward, square your hips to the front (toward an imaginary opponent) and raise your right knee to your chest. This is called "chambering" the kick. Bringing the knee to the chest this way protects your groin and lower torso from attack as you prepare to kick. Chambering also helps you keep your balance after you kick, so that you can kick again effectively with the same foot or, maintaining your balance,

place the foot down where you choose. If you don't re-chamber a kick, you will likely have to put your foot down wherever it lands to keep your balance, and this leaves you vulnerable.

Extend the kick toward the imaginary target. The front kick's weapon is the ball of the foot, so as you extend the kick, draw the toes back toward you to expose the ball of the foot and point the foot

To perform a rear-leg front kick, start in a ready position with the left leg forward.

down a little. This position gives you a little more reach on the kick. Bring the kick back into chamber (knee at your chest), and then place the leg down in the starting position.

This example illustrates a front kick with the rear leg, but lead-leg front kicks can be very effective when they are used as a jab. In kickboxing, front-leg kicks are used more often as a jab than are jabs with the lead hand. This is because boxing-like hand jabs are ineffective against a good kicker. Lead-leg front kicks used as jabs can keep an opponent away or catch a blitzing or hand-jabbing opponent in the stomach or ribs as he moves toward you. A lead-leg front kick can also be used to begin a variety of punching and kicking combinations.

The front kick targets just about any area from the head to the lower abdomen.

If you're new to kicking, including each step in this kick as you practice—especially chambering—is vital. More advanced kickboxers might

Square your hips to the front (toward an imaginary opponent) and raise your right knee to your chest. This is called "chambering" the kick. Bringing the knee to the chest this way protects your groin and lower torso from attack as you prepare to kick. Chambering also helps you keep your balance after you kick.

extend the kick toward the imaginary target. The front kick's weapon is the ball of the foot, so as you extend the kick, draw the toes back toward you to expose the ball of the foot and point the foot down a little. This position gives you a little more reach on the kick.

appear to be skipping some steps when they kick, but they aren't. Front kicks are chambered when they are performed with either the forward leg or the rear leg.

In addition, if you're new to kicking, train and condition the muscles around the toes to bend the toes back and expose the ball-of-the-foot weapon.

One way to accomplish this is to walk around the training area every day for a few minutes on the balls of your feet.

As you practice the kick, remember to keep the guard up.

In kickboxing, as in traditional Taekwondo competition, you must displace an opponent with a kick to score a point, so you need to put a little forward hip action into the front kick as you fire it out. Otherwise, you might only touch your opponent with a weak and easily parried leg extension. In some traditional martial-arts schools, this kick is called a front snap kick, but for kickboxing, it's more of a thrusting kick, meant to drive an opponent backward.

then place the leg down in the starting position.

bring the kick back into chamber (knee at your chest).

Football Kick

A football kick is a kind of front kick, but the weapon is the instep. When the opponent covers up, bobs down, or crunches over and leans forward, the football kick might work. You step back and strike the opponent in the face with the rear-leg instep. Even if the opponent has his forearms in front of his face, you can still hurt the opponent. This kick doesn't require much flexibility, and it's a very powerful kick with the rear leg.

To perform it properly, with your right leg back, raise the leg in chamber as if you were performing a front kick. Bend the foot down and curl the toes downward to prepare the instep weapon. From a chambered position, execute the kick. Chambering isn't always necessary with this kick. Twisting the hips slightly to the left adds to its power.

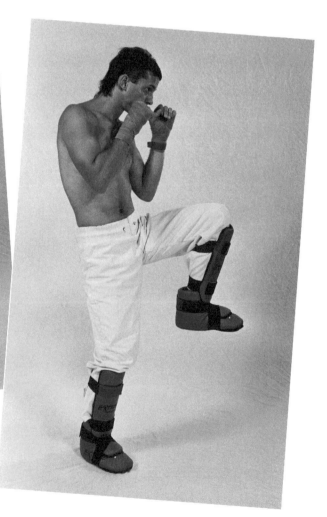

to perform a football kick with the rear (right) leg, start in a fighting stance with the left foot forward.

raise the leg in chamber as if you were performing a front kick. Bend the foot down and curl the toes downward to prepare the instep weapon.

from a chambered position, execute the kick. Chambering isn't always necessary with this kick. Twisting the hips slightly to the left adds to its power. The weapon is the instep.

bring the leg back into chamber.

return to the starting position.

Roundhouse Kick

There are three slightly different kinds of roundhouse kicks that are used most often in kickboxing. The first kind is the instep roundhouse, with which most martial art students are already familiar. This roundhouse's weapon is the talus, a bone at the top of the instep (ankle).

To perform an instep roundhouse kick with the right rear leg, from a ready position with the left leg forward, square the hips to the front (toward an imaginary opponent) and raise the rear (right) leg into chamber. As you chamber the leg, prepare the instep weapon by pointing the toes downward, exposing the instep. Pivot the hips toward the left, almost straight toward the target, and extend the kick. Bring the kick back into chamber, turning the hips toward the right (square again), and then place the foot down in the starting position.

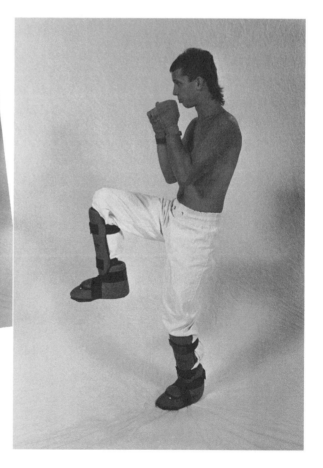

to perform an instep roundhouse kick with the right rear leg, begin in a fighting position with the left leg forward.

Square the hips to the front (toward an imaginary opponent) and raise the rear (right) leg into chamber.

as you chamber the leg, prepare the instep weapon by pointing the toes downward, exposing the instep. Pivot the hips toward the left, almost straight toward the target.

extend the kick.

bring the kick back into chamber, turning the hips toward the right (square again).

place the foot down in the starting position. The instep roundhouse kick's power comes from the snapping motion and torque of the hips turning as the kick is delivered.

The instep roundhouse kick's power comes from the snapping motion and torque of the hips turning as the kick is delivered.

This kick can also be performed with the front leg. If you have the flexibility, speed, and power, a front-leg roundhouse to the opponent's head can be effective. Other targets include the abdominal area and the legs, where leg kicks are permitted.

The next roundhouse kick is the ball-of-the-foot roundhouse. Its weapon is the ball of the foot—the same weapon as the front kick. Perform this roundhouse as you execute the instep roundhouse kick, but you don't produce as much torque and twisting power with this kick as you generate with the instep roundhouse kick. When performed quickly, this kick is useful for attacking the abdominal area of an opponent who is well-guarded. The fist-like weapon of the ball of the foot turned inward can often penetrate a well-defended opponent.

The third roundhouse kick, the powerful straight-leg roundhouse, uses the shin as the weapon. To perform a rear-leg straight-leg roundhouse, from a fighting position with the left leg forward, bring the right leg up without chambering, in one quick motion. Point the toes downward as you would in performing an instep roundhouse. This kick is designed to generate a lot of power as you torque the hips and deliver the kick. This roundhouse is used in competitions in which leg kicks are allowed, like Muay Thai (see Chapter 7).

Eliminating the chamber in this kick takes away much of

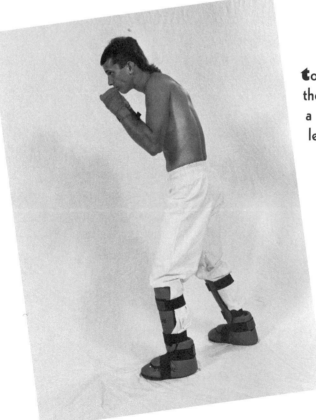

To perform an ax kick with the right (rear) leg, start in a fighting stance with the left leg forward.

the telegraphing of the kick that chambering sometimes provides. This kick targets the lower legs, inner thigh area, and hamstrings. A low kick like this is difficult to see coming and block. This kick is very powerful once you condition the nerves of the shins; then this kick is like striking with a baseball bat.

Ax Kick

The ax kick's weapon is the heel. The leg's high chopping motion gives this kick its name. Performing an ax kick effectively calls for plenty of speed and power. You have to get the leg up high fast and bring it down forcefully on the target. Working with a partner holding focus pads can help you develop this power and speed.

Performing an ax kick might seem easy, but this kick is not simple to execute, especially with a skilled, alert opponent. Hiding the preparation of a rear-leg ax kick is very difficult, so it's best to work the technique as a front-leg kick.

To perform an ax kick with the rear leg—the right leg in this example—start in the fighting stance with the left leg forward. As you raise the leg, turn the hips toward the left. Don't chamber the knee, but do bend it slightly. Raise the leg in a slight arc, angling slightly to a point above the target. As you begin chopping down onto the target, twist the hips to the right. The kick can also be performed by arcing the leg from the outside in, but this way is a bit cumbersome.

The ax kick can be used primarily to attack the head, shoulders, and chest. This kick has to be set up in combination with other kicks and punches. Don't use it as a single kick.

As you raise the leg, turn the hips toward the left. Don't chamber the knee, but do bend it slightly. Raise the leg in a slight arc, angling slightly to a point above the target. As you begin chopping down onto the target, twist the hips to the right. The kick can also be performed by arcing the leg from the outside in, but this way is a bit cumbersome.

Side Kick

The side kick can be a powerful weapon when performed with the rear leg. A front-leg side kick can be used as a jab. It can also be effective when you catch a jabbing opponent, or an opponent who punches a lot, in the ribs. The side kick's weapon is the blade of the foot at the heel. Don't focus on using the entire blade of the foot as this kick's weapon. That makes a "mushy" kick, and dissipates the kick's power. Think of the weapon as a spot on the heel, as if the weapon were the end of a ball peen hammer—a small, focused striking area.

To perform a rear-leg side kick, from a fighting position with the left leg forward, raise the right leg into chamber, turning the hips square toward the front (toward an imaginary opponent). Prepare the weapon as you chamber this kick by raising the chambered leg's toes and pointing the blade of the foot downward. Turn the hips to the left, nearly in a side position, keeping the kicking leg in chamber. Extend the kick. Bring the kicking leg back into chamber with the hips still in a side position. Return to the starting position.

raise the right leg into chamber, turning the hips square toward the front (toward an imaginary opponent). Prepare the weapon as you chamber the kick by raising the chambered leg's toes and pointing the blade of the foot downward.

to perform a rear-leg (right) side kick, begin in a fighting position with the left leg forward.

turn the hips to the left, nearly in a side position, keeping the kicking leg in chamber.

extend the kick.

bring the kicking leg back into chamber with the hips still in a side position.

return to the starting position.

Hook Kick

This kick's weapon is the heel. The hook kick can be performed with either leg. If you're fast and flexible, a lead-leg hook kick to the head can be effective in combination with other techniques. A rear-leg hook kick can be powerful, but you have to perform it quickly. It's best to set up a rear-leg hook kick with other techniques.

To execute a lead-leg hook kick, start with the left leg forward. Raise the kick into chamber, bringing the knee to your chest. Turn the hips to the right. Fire out the kick as if you were performing a side kick. Just before the kick reaches the target, hook the leg to the left, as if you were grabbing the target with your foot. After following through, re-chamber the leg and return it to the starting position.

To execute a lead-leg hook kick, start in a fighting position with the left leg forward.

Raise the kick into chamber, bringing the knee to your chest, and turn the hips to the right.

fire out the kick as if you were performing a side kick. Just before the kick reaches the target, hook the leg to the left, as if you were grabbing the target with your foot.

after following through, re-chamber the leg and return it to the starting position.

Spinning Kicks

To execute a spinning back kick, or a spinning hook kick, start in a fighting stance. Turn the body and head so that you can see the target. Bring the kicking leg into chamber. From this position, begin the kick. The torque you create from spinning quickly adds more power to these kicks than stationary kicks. The placement of the feet for the spinning hook kick and spinning back kick is the same. However, when you execute a spinning hook kick, as the kick nears its full extension, hook it inward, as if you were grabbing the target with your foot.

Spinning kicks are much more difficult to perform than stationary kicks. To be effective, you must develop great speed, power, and accuracy with these techniques. You must also learn to defend quickly after you execute these kicks. An alert fighter can quickly spot an ineffective spinning kick. He'll either jam the kick (be all over you before you perform the kick) or attack after he makes you miss.

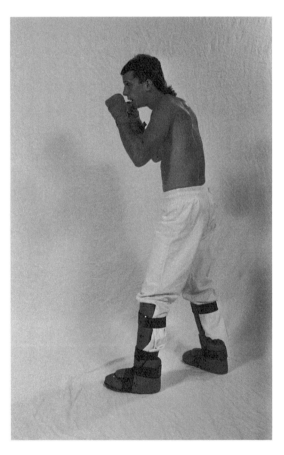

turn the body and head so that you can see the target.

to execute a spinning back kick with the rear (right) leg, start in a fighting stance.

bring the kicking leg into chamber.

from this position, begin the kick. The torque you create from spinning quickly adds more power to these kicks than stationary kicks.

place the leg down and return to the fighting stance.

Kicking Drills

After you learn the basic execution of each kick, practice them in drills. Repetition helps you ingrain techniques so that you don't have to think about them to perform them correctly.

Heavy Bag

Practicing kicking techniques on a heavy bag can help you learn timing. When you kick the bag, it moves. When the bag moves back into range, as an opponent would move, kick it again. Move around the bag as you'd fight an opponent.

Two-Person Reaction Drill

This strenuous drill helps you maintain good kicking form, increase kicking speed, and decrease reaction time. These qualities are important because when you see an opening in your opponent's defense, you must take advantage of the opportunity quickly.

You and a partner face each other. Your partner throws a roundhouse kick. You block

and immediately fire back with a roundhouse kick. Your partner blocks and kicks back. This drill also helps you remember to keep your guard up while you kick.

Speed Drill

Your coach or training partner holds a kicking shield, while you and another partner stand on either side. You throw a

Practicing kicking techniques on a heavy bag can help you learn timing. When you kick the bag, it moves. When the bag moves back into range, as an opponent would move, kick it again. Move around the bag as you'd fight an opponent.

roundhouse kick. As soon as you finish, your partner kicks, and you kick again immediately after your partner kicks. This drill helps you increase your kicking accuracy while maintaining good form. This drill is very physically demanding, as is the two-person reaction drill. However, the benefit of learning to maintain accuracy and form is vital, especially when you tire.

Power Drill

Your coach or training partner holds a kicking shield. You kick, and your coach moves around, changing the angles and positions from which you must kick to hit the target. Each kick should be as powerful as you can muster. This drill is useful with all your kicks. It helps you learn the best angles from which all your kicks are effective.

In a power drill, you kick, and your coach moves around, changing the angles and positions from which you must kick to hit the target. Each kick should be as powerful as you can muster. This drill is useful with all your kicks. It helps you learn the best angles from which all your kicks are effective.

FRONT-LEG SWEEP

In full-contact karate, sweeping the front (lead) leg is allowed, but you must attack the lead leg only from the outside. Sweeping the support (rear) leg is not allowed. The idea with a sweep in kickboxing is to knock the opponent off balance—you don't have to put someone on the canvas. Your opponent is open to your attack when he is off balance, even for an instant. In fact, even if you do knock the opponent to the canvas with your sweep, amateur and professional rules don't consider going to the canvas as a result of a sweep a knockdown.

When you're close to your opponent, the feet have to be close together so you can move side to side and gain leverage in your punches. Standing farther away, as a good kicker might, the legs can be farther apart in a wider stance. It's easier to sweep an opponent's lead leg when his feet are farther apart than close together. When the opponent's feet are farther apart, the opponent must distribute his weight evenly. When the feet are closer together, he is better balanced and can evade a sweep simply by lifting the front leg. Fighters who favor wide, open stances in close—like those of some traditional karate styles—are open to sweeps.

Perform a sweep either with the front or the rear leg. One way to execute a sweep is to perform a very low instep roundhouse kick. Another method is to use the bottom of the foot. Remember that both techniques must attack the lead leg from the outside. Practice sweeps with follow-up punching combinations.

Sweeps are most effective when they are set up. Sweeping a well-guarded opponent as a lead technique is not often successful. If you can kick your opponent and make contact often, even if your kicks are blocked, you might be able to divert the opponent's attention with mid-level and high techniques, and then target the lead leg with a sweep.

A successful sweep unbalances the opponent. This means that the opponent most often momentarily plants both feet solidly on the ground and lowers the guard. This opening in the opponent's defense is why you should practice sweeping with follow-up techniques.

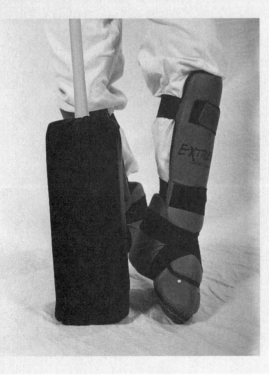

Perform a sweep either with the front or the rear leg. One way to execute a sweep is to perform a very low instep roundhouse kick. Practice with blocking equipment. Have a partner hold the device more firmly on the floor as you gain skill.

If you sweep your opponent, you might also be the target of a sweep. To defend against a sweep, keep moving unpredictably. If your opponent knows you can sweep successfully, he might be hesitant to kick. Add this consideration to your strategy.

Before a fight, research your opponent's background to see if his coaches teach and encourage sweeps, and if the opponent has used them before. From this, you may determine the likelihood of an opponent's using this technique.

Tension Kicking

Perform this drill by holding on to a bar or chair back for support. Perform all your kicks very slowly in this drill. Go through each step of each kick and hold each step a few seconds. Perform all your kicks three or four times with each leg this way. This drill helps you build flexibility, strength, and technique.

Back-and-Forth Drills

With a partner or your coach, you kick, with one kind of kick at first and then in combinations of different kicks. Your coach moves straight back at first, and then in random directions. This exercise helps you learn to kick effectively from different angles, and you learn the distances from which you can kick effectively.

Perform tension kicking drills by holding on to a bar or chair back for support and balance. Perform all your kicks very slowly in this drill. Go through each step of each kick and hold each step about five seconds. This drill helps you build flexibility, strength, and technique.

chapter five

RING SKILLS

Learning ring skills starts at the beginning of your kickboxing training, but performing these techniques well is an advanced skill. Still, using ring skills effectively can mean the difference between winning and losing. Do not underestimate this idea. If you don't train regularly in a regulation-size ring as you prepare for your first fight, do so.

A ring is different from a wood or cement floor. A ring has a one-inch cushion, so it is a lot "slower" than other harder surfaces, and it wears you out much faster than the harder-surfaced training area you might be accustomed to. You must get used to moving in the ring, and accustomed to the footing. That calls for a lot of ring work—and that means doing everything in your training in the ring.

Fighters with little ring experience always seem to get

Learning ring skills starts at the beginning of your kickboxing training, but performing these techniques well is an advanced skill. Still, using ring skills effectively can mean the difference between winning and losing.

If you don't train regularly in a regulation-size ring as you prepare for your first fight, do so. A ring is different from a wood or cement floor. A ring has a one-inch cushion, so it's a lot "slower" than other harder surfaces, and it wears you out much faster than the harder-surfaced training area you might be accustomed to. You have to get used to moving in the ring, and get accustomed to the footing.

rope burns from rubbing up against the ring ropes. Beginners who train in a ring are often more conditioned with toughened skin. Rope burns often appear to be marks from punches and kicks. Fighters with little ring experience can appear to the judges to be taking more of a beating than they actually are. These fighters also slip and fall often because they are not accustomed to the ring's footing.

A regulation-size ring is from 16 feet to 26 feet inside the ropes, corner to corner, with four ropes not higher than 46 inches.

Cutting Off the Ring

When you cut off the ring, you maneuver an opponent toward a corner or to the ropes to strike with power punches and

kicks. Through movement, you continually work side and side, and quickly and strategically eliminate the opponent's escape routes. Slowly that person moves backward until there is no other place to move. Think of this technique as "corralling" the opponent.

To cut off the ring, work the jab and leg on one side, and then work the other side, striking back and forth. As the opponent tries to avoid your attacks, he moves backward and away from the direction of the punches and kicks. It's easier to maneuver a fatigued fighter this way than it is to corner a fresh opponent.

You cut off the ring by zigzagging an opponent into the ropes or into a corner. A corner is difficult to get out of, and it's easier to keep a fatigued opponent there. There are no ropes to bounce off, just pole padding. Getting out of a corner becomes more of a physical battle, and that's even more difficult for a tired opponent.

If you find yourself in a corner, parry the opponent's right-hand punches with your left arm and step to your left to spin away. Then the opponent must turn and find you again before he can go on the offensive.

Similarly, you could step under the attack, turning the opponent around. Suppose the opponent throws a jab and right cross. You bob underneath the attack so that your head is almost right against his belly. When he throws the right hand, your head will be underneath his armpit. Put your right hand around him and push him out of the way. This maneuver is difficult, but it's important to learn and practice.

What if your opponent is trying to corral you? To defeat the opponent's cutting off the ring, you could attack straight at the opponent to move him backward and away. Cutting off the ring and defending against it then becomes a strategic contest. With this strategy it can boil down to which opponent is quicker and stronger.

If you find yourself in a corner or on the ropes, parry the opponent's right-hand punches with your left arm and step to your left to spin away. Then the opponent must turn and find you again before he can go on the offensive.

learn to circle away from your opponent's power (away from the rear arm and rear leg). Practice this important ring skill in the ring with a partner. As you work with your coach or partner, circle to your right with a right-handed fighter (arrows), and to your left with a lefty.

Another option to defeat your opponent's cutting off the ring is to drill and get into the habit of taking no more than two steps backward and then circling. Chances are, when you take two steps back from the center of the ring, you're near the ropes, anyway. This strategy makes cutting off the ring difficult for your opponent, and it makes you a more difficult target to hit. A fighter who moves straight backward all the time is an easy target.

Practice this important skill in the ring with a partner. As you work with your coach or partner wearing focus mitts, circle to your right with a right-handed fighter, and to the left with a lefty. The idea is to circle away from the opponent's power. As you prepare for a fight, your coach can tell you whether the opponent fights right-handed or left-handed. Practice circling both left and right, but work more on circling away from your next opponent's power.

If you notice your opponent trying to cut off the ring in a

fighters need to be taught ring skills correctly. No one expects a beginner to perform flawlessly. In fact, even with adequate preparation, a beginner does not apply much of the ring skills he's learned because of nerves and excitement during those first few fights. Having the knowledge is one thing; experience raises your skill level.

predictable pattern, you can use that pattern to set him up with powerful defensive techniques.

Bouncing off the ropes is another useful skill. You and your coach can work this drill with focus pads. Your coach will occasionally push you into the ropes and ask for certain responses. Your coach might hold the mitts high for a punching combination as you bounce off the ropes, or he might hold the mitts lower for a roundhouse combination. This is a reaction drill. As you bounce off the ropes, you need to react to whatever the opponent presents. Your opponent will likely want to punch you as you bounce off the ropes. You must learn first to hold your hands up to protect your head when you bounce off the ropes.

On the Ropes

To keep someone on the ropes, use your body. A physically stronger fighter can find it easier to keep an opponent against the ropes. A fatigued fighter can't work off the ropes as easily.

To come off the ropes, move or "roll" off the ropes as you block or parry a punch or kick. Move with the block of a punch or with the direction of the kick to turn the opponent onto the ropes, or to move yourself into the center of the ring.

Ring skills are like punching and kicking skills. Drill the individual techniques first, and then put them into an application in the ring. Learning these skills comes through training and experience, and lots of both.

Fighters also need to be taught correctly. No one expects a beginner to perform flawlessly. In fact, even with adequate preparation, a beginner does not apply much of the ring skills he's learned because of nerves and excitement during those first few fights. Having the knowledge is one thing; experience raises your skill level.

This is why it's important to train in the ring. You can probably develop some of these skills in an open training area. But training in the ring is different.

Furthermore, you hone ring skills through foot movement. The more aware you are of the ring, and where you are in the ring, the more you can move skillfully in the ring.

chapter six

FIGHTING STRATEGIES

As you gain a strong foundation in kickboxing's basic techniques, you learn how to put combinations of kicks and punches together in an effective, strategic way. You also learn to create openings in the opponent's defense, that is, to set up the opponent, and follow up on an opponent's mistakes, where the opponent has created an opening for you. You have an advantage when you can effectively throw a series of combinations where any one technique or combination of techniques will hurt the opponent. You learn these techniques through experience and continued training.

As you are advancing, all of your training goes back to foundation. That's why it's vital to establish a strong foundation to build on. It's possible that one kick or one punch could drop your opponent, but you don't want to go into the ring thinking that's the way it's going to be. Remember that your opponent is also a trained fighter. You need to go into the ring thoroughly prepared, believing that to put combinations together, even to hit the opponent, you're going to have to work hard.

By the time you achieve these goals, you are beyond the basics. You're working on all the techniques you need to fight in the ring.

Kicks, Punches

Take single kicks and put them in combinations. Look first at how the body moves. The easiest way to break a piece of wood, for instance, is to go with the grain. If you throw a kick in which the momentum of your body is going in one direction and the next kick goes in the other direction, you slow up, and there has to be hesitation in the combination. Going against the grain, like performing a front-leg side kick and then with the other leg coming around with an ax kick, creates more movement and it's cumbersome. The combination does not flow. Performing a front-leg roundhouse kick into a spinning back kick with the other leg is a more fluid motion.

Punching combinations also need to flow. Punching with the right arm twice, for instance, is time-consuming, even though it's a combination that could work when set up in some circumstances. But for the beginner, those two punches could be more effective if they were a jab–right cross combination. You're creating an opening and one punch follows the other faster.

few fighters can throw more than five techniques in a combination at top speed without losing power. Practice combinations of your favorite and most effective techniques. Begin this combination in a fighting stance with the left foot forward. Start with a left-leg snap kick . . .

left jab,

right cross, and

right-leg roundhouse.

here's another combination you might find effective. Start with a left jab . . .

right cross,

right-leg roundhouse kick, and

left-leg front kick. You get the idea with combinations. Let your technique flow from side to side, fast and powerfully, mixing punches and kicks. Practice the combinations right-left/right-left, high-low/high-low, punch-kick/punch-kick.

Because of individual differences in flexibility and body types, work on the combinations you use most effectively. Your coach will help you identify these techniques. Don't work on everything you know. Over time, the complexity of your kicking and punching combinations will grow. At the beginning, just work a few combinations and develop them so that you feel comfortable and can use them without thinking about them. By working only a few combinations, you will be more likely to use those combinations effectively in the stressful situation of a fight.

Few fighters can throw more than five techniques in a combination at top speed without losing power. The whole idea in putting combinations together is to punch and kick all the time at 100 percent efficiency. After five techniques, that efficiency drops quickly. Remember also that in the ring, if you throw too many kicks in a row, you're simply going to run out of room. This means that you should practice three to five techniques in your combinations, and then back off.

Below are several basic combinations you can try. Even though there are any number of combinations you could create, let these few give you an idea of how effective combinations flow. Practice them for a while, and then modify them to suit your ability, or create new ones that let you use your favorite and most effective techniques. Begin all of these combinations in a fighting stance with the left foot forward.

You get the idea—let your technique flow from side to side, fast and powerfully, mixing punches and kicks. Practice combinations right-left/right-left, high-low/high-low, punch-kick/punch-kick. End each flurry with a jab or side kick—a retreating technique that lets you move backward and create distance between you and the opponent without opening yourself up to an attack. This drilling also helps you fight unpredictably. Unpredictability makes it difficult for your opponent to set you up.

Walking Drills

Begin learning combinations with walking drills, first only with hand techniques, then only kicks, and then putting these together. In a walking drill, you move the length of the training area back and forth, performing the techniques. Start with moving non-contact air techniques. Then with a partner, try using kicking shields and focus pads. Progress from walking drills to bag work, in which you're making physical contact, advancing finally to facing an opponent.

With the right foot forward, try a right-hand jab, left-hand cross, left-foot roundhouse, right-foot roundhouse as a walking drill. You might also try two or three jabs, a round-

❏ Left-leg snap kick, left jab, right cross, right-leg roundhouse.

❏ Right-leg roundhouse, left-leg roundhouse, left jab, straight right, right snap kick.

❏ Left jab, right cross, left jab, right-leg snap kick, left jab.

❏ Left jab, right cross, left hook, right uppercut, left jab.

❏ Left jab, right cross, right-leg roundhouse kick, left-leg front kick.

house, and a side kick. There are countless combinations that can work. The key is discovering the offensive and countering combos that are most effective for you—your style and abilities.

Stances

Footwork is important because that's how you learn to move in the ring, and footwork lets you maximize your power for punching and kicking. For instance, when you are out of range of your opponent, the feet can be farther apart. When you're close to your opponent and your feet are far apart, it's easy for him to sweep your lead leg and knock you off balance. So when you're close to someone, use punching techniques with the feet closer together. When your feet are closer together, you can move side to side faster and you can put more leverage in your punches.

Countering

Learning to counter various attacks is also important. You learn to counter with the same training drills you use for the offense. For example, with a kicking shield, your partner or coach moves toward you, as if the shield were the opponent's body. Your coach or partner, simulating an opponent, puts on protective gear and throws techniques, and you react. In a two-kick combination, for instance, try cutting off the second kick. Block the kick and quickly close the distance to the opponent with a punching combination.

Suppose your training partner or coach tries a series of rear-leg roundhouse kicks. Practice blocking and countering with a series of punches.

You can practice any number of counterattacks in reaction drills—your partner throws the technique and you practice countering. The drill is performed repeatedly around the ring or training area. Apply the same drill for punching counterattacks.

Fighting Strategy

When you're preparing for your first fight, you might be able to study films or tapes of the opponent. This is part of learning how to "read" your opponent. You need to assess whether the opponent will come with a kick, a punch, with the front arm or leg, or with the back leg or arm. A lot of the opponent's intentions can be determined by learning to read an opponent's shoulders. If a person is trying to fake you out by jutting the arms or shoulders, through experience you learn to read this ploy. Then, as an opponent starts to fake and play, a more seasoned fighter can counter quickly and effectively.

Faking can be effective for new fighters, but as you gain experience, you can defeat it. Gaining experience is part of developing a fighting strategy. It takes time to effectively read an opponent.

You learn to protect against punching with a lot of movement. The head should be moving constantly. The more controlled movement you have, the harder you are to hit, and if you do get hit, it's less likely the strike will be a direct, devastating blow. Keep a good, solid guard up to deflect attacks if the opponent is quick.

Another way to defend against strong punches and kicks is always to circle away from your opponent's power. This forces your opponent either to telegraph his most powerful techniques with added movement to reach you, or strike less powerfully and awkwardly.

learn to block with the elbows and shoulders. To do this, try this drill. Your partner (right) first performs a left jab, which you parry with your right hand.

then he throws a right cross, which you parry with your left hand.

as he comes around with a left hook, raise the right elbow, as if you were just showing the opponent your underarm. Practice this parry-parry-elbow block in left-right-left and right-left-right combinations.

DISCOVERING YOUR STRENGTHS AND WEAKNESSES

E xperience and continued training let you discover your strengths and weaknesses. The best plan is to keep practicing all areas, but try to draw the opponent into fighting your fight.

For instance, suppose you're fighting a "slugger" or a "banger." This fighter prefers to stand in the middle of the ring and pound it out, using more power than speed. He'll wait in the middle of the ring for you to come to him, or he'll try to draw you there. He'll also try to maneuver you against the ropes, where he can just pound away. If he can't maneuver you into a corner, he may go to the body with powerful strikes to slow you down and fatigue you.

On the other hand, you might be fighting a "boxer." This opponent focuses on speed and movement. He sticks and moves, sticks and moves, using combinations to wear you down and out-point you.

If either fighter can anger or frustrate you because you can't make the opponent fight "your fight," you may fall into the trap of losing your concentration. Then you may open yourself to being knocked out.

Which fighter are you?

What are your strengths?

Kicking? Punching? Speed? Power? Remember that in training for your first fight, you work on all these areas to avoid being a one-dimensional fighter. Experience will help you discover your strengths and weaknesses. You will likely discover that in your first few fights the most important quality is endurance. Then you work on controlling your nerves in the ring.

You should also learn to block with the elbows and shoulders. To do this, try this drill. Your partner performs a left jab, which you parry with your right hand. Then he throws a right cross, which you parry with your left hand. As he comes around with a left hook, raise the right elbow, as if you were just showing the opponent your underarm. Practice this parry-parry-elbow block in left-right-left and right-left-right combinations.

"Covering up" means getting the guard up—elbows in, to protect the ribs, fists up near the forehead to protect the face, and chin tucked in. Covering up lets you defend momentarily against a flurry of punches and kicks. Against the ropes, covering up means going into this cocoon-like posture to hide vulnerable spots. This is the time you can regain composure and not get hit.

Remember that your main strategy is to beat the opponent—not necessarily knock him out. You fight trying to set him up at first, and ultimately—if possible—knock him out. Every fighter should plan to go into every fight to go the distance, and should prepare accordingly. But it's also important to know when you've actually hurt the opponent and then go in for a knockout.

If you just try for a knockout, you're looking for that one kick or one punch. Then you're depending on luck, or that you're so much better than the opponent. Most of the time, fighters are evenly matched. Go into the fight thinking you're going to outfight the opponent, and if the opportunity arises, knock him out. Remember that the fight is only two or three rounds, and that the winner is determined by the total points each fighter accrues. These rules encourage fighters to be skilled and well conditioned.

The winning combination includes both brains and brawn. You should map out a strategy with adequate physical preparation. Most champion kickboxers have extensive amateur backgrounds. Their foundations were established in the amateur ranks. This kind of preparation requires training three to five times a week for three to six months for someone who already has a solid martial-arts or boxing background. Kickboxing calls for applying that boxing or martial-arts experience in a different way.

chapter seven

TYPES OF KICKBOXING

Generally speaking, there are three main kinds of kickboxing: full-contact karate, kickboxing, and Muay Thai.

Full-contact karate is the kind of kickboxing most Americans do. All punches and kicks must be above the waist. No elbow or knee techniques are allowed. Lead-leg sweeps are sometimes allowed. (Sweeps are viewed as a separate group of techniques—they aren't considered kicks.) No other leg kicks are allowed. Mandatory equipment usually includes headgear, gloves, mouthpiece, groin guard, and foot and shin protectors.

Kickboxing, a little different from full-contact karate, allows kicks to the legs. In this kind of kickboxing, roundhouse kicks to the backs of the legs and inner thighs are common. Variations of this leg-kick rule are also common.

Muay Thai, also called Thai boxing, is the national sport of Thailand. (Credit: Vincent Soberano)

muay Thai fighters, like other kickboxers, use modern Western-style boxing gloves, with no shin guards or foot guards. (Credit: Vincent Soberano)

What eventually became known as Muay Thai is probably about a thousand years old. Muay Thai was most likely used as military combat training in what was then Siam. Muay Thai allows kicks, punches, knee strikes, and elbow strikes anywhere except the groin. Some grabbing and holding techniques are also permitted. Matches last five rounds, three minutes per round, with a two-minute rest period between rounds. Muay Thai fighters, like other kickboxers, use modern Western-style boxing gloves.

Licensing, Rules

There are many kickboxing sanctioning organizations in the United States and around the world. These organizations set the rules and procedures that govern fights. The laws concerning who has to be licensed in kickboxing vary from state to state. Some state laws group kickboxing with boxing. Some states don't. You and your coach need to make certain all the legal and licensing details are in order for your participation and training. Licensing often requires showing proof of insurance and of being bonded. Initially, this can be expensive. Contact your state's athletic commission or department of state to be certain who has to be licensed and how to fulfill the require-

Contact your state's athletic commission or department of state to be certain who has to be licensed and how to fulfill the requirements. Promoters, trainers, managers, gyms, matchmakers, referees, judges, timekeepers, cornermen, ring physicians, announcers, and fighters all may have to be licensed in your state. (Credit: Vincent Soberano)

ments. Promoters, trainers, managers, gyms, matchmakers, referees, judges, timekeepers, cornermen, ring physicians, announcers, and fighters all may have to be licensed in your state.

Legalities and licensing aside, you may not find the same rules for the same event in one place as you'd find in another place. For instance, in one organization in which leg kicks are allowed, kicks only to the outside of the legs might be permitted, with no kicks allowed to the insides of the legs. In other fights, inside and outside leg kicks are permitted. In still other areas, outside leg kicks may be permitted but only above the knees. When leg kicks are permitted, they must be at least six inches above or below the knee. Fighters are trained this way, too. Rules that include leg kicks often specify that kicks are not allowed to the joints.

Furthermore, where sweeps are allowed, some organizations permit sweeps to the inside or outside of the lead leg. Sometimes, sweeps are permitted to the lead leg only from the outside. These sweeps are called "boot to boot."

Sweeps can be dangerous, so coaches, promoters, and fighters need to be clear on what's permitted and what's not allowed. Rear-leg sweeps, double-leg sweeps, and other sweep-like kicks and takedowns—common in self-defense training—are meant to take an opponent's feet out from under him. Sweeps in kickboxing are meant only to unbalance an opponent momentarily to set up other punches and kicks.

Because you will find great variety in the rules governing fights, make sure you and your coach are thoroughly familiar with the rules under which you're going to fight. You need to gear your training to these rules. At least a month before a fight, it's wise to focus your training and practice under the set of rules of that fight. In this way, you can minimize the chances of being penalized or disqualified for breaking the rules.

If you do break the rules, you are most often warned the first time. The second infraction often causes a deduction in points. The third violation will probably get you disqualified. You might also be disqualified on the first infraction if the violation injures your opponent.

Depending on the geographical area, one sanction and set of rules may be more popular than another. It is important to identify these different rules, such as international rules (with leg kicks) versus American rules (no leg kicks). Amateur kickboxers compete under both rules, depending sometimes on their location. For example, in southern California and Mexico, you will hardly find any kickboxing events that do not allow leg kicks. In northern California and the eastern United States, however, American rules are more popular.

Amateur competitors are divided into weight classes in all these kinds of kickboxing. In the amateur ranks, though, the weight classes are somewhat larger than in boxing, especially in exhibition fights. In amateur title fights and in the professional ranks, fixed matches are set between fighters in the same weight classes.

In the amateur ranks, non-title fights are arranged this way, too, but many exhibition fights are sometimes made by matching fighters according to weight and experience. In these fights, competitors aren't supposed to be trying to knock each other out. These fights are geared more toward letting the fighters gain ring experience. They're basically sparring in front of an audience.

Exhibition fights often apply to physically challenged fighters and perhaps older fighters or those kickboxers who want to fight but who are not conditioned enough for more formal matching with an opponent. Exhibition fights are also undertaken when amateurs cannot arrange to compete with someone in their weight

at least a month before a fight, you'll focus hard on training under the rules of the fight, especially if the rules are different from what you're used to.

class. Both fighters in an exhibition match still benefit from the experience. These kinds of matches and tournaments are organized with the flavors of both open karate tournaments and more formal matching of fighters. Rules concerning leg kicks and other requirements are usually confirmed during matchmaking.

In the amateur ranks, the number of rounds and their length depend on the experience of the fighter. If you're inexperienced, with three fights or fewer, your fights will probably be two or three rounds of 1½ to 2 minutes. With more experience, your fights will probably include five 2-minute rounds, and with still more experience, you might fight five 3-minute rounds.

An ideal schedule includes a fight every month. In many places, however, a fight once a month isn't practical. You will probably find that fighting once every two months is a more appropriate goal that would help keep you in good condition.

WEIGHT CLASSES

■■■

Weights in these classes are approximate, but here's what you probably will find:

Atomweight
117 pounds and less

Flyweight
Over 117 pounds to 120 pounds

Bantamweight
Over 120 pounds to 124 pounds

Featherweight
Over 124 pounds to 128 pounds

Lightweight
Over 128 pounds to 132 pounds

Super Lightweight
Over 132 pounds to 137 pounds

Light Welterweight
Over 137 pounds to 142 pounds

Welterweight
Over 142 pounds to 147 pounds

Super Welterweight
Over 147 pounds to 153 pounds

Light Middleweight
Over 153 pounds to 159 pounds

Middleweight
Over 159 pounds to 165 pounds

Super Middleweight
Over 165 pounds to 172 pounds

Light Heavyweight
Over 172 pounds to 179 pounds

Light Cruiserweight
Over 179 pounds to 186 pounds

Cruiserweight
Over 186 pounds to 195 pounds

Heavyweight
Over 195 to 215 pounds

Super Heavyweight
Over 215 pounds

Strategy

If you plan to fight with leg kicks, you must train using leg kicks, incorporating them into your strategy. Combinations work off leg kicks just as combinations in boxing, karate, and full-contact karate are designed to create openings in an opponent's defense (see Chapter 6).

For example, one combination includes a front-leg inside leg kick, rear-leg outside leg kick, and left hook punch. Kicking the outside of the leg turns the opponent away and causes him to drop the guard, opening the opponent to a hook punch.

Another effective combination includes a roundhouse kick to the outside of the leg and a roundhouse to the inside of the leg. This squares the opponent to you, in which case he's open to a powerful rear-leg front kick.

The important training strategy is that you must incorporate all the legal tactics. Like all other skills, you learn the individual techniques

Kickboxing training in all styles, like other martial arts training, can begin at an early age. (Credit: Vincent Soberano)

and drill them separately. Then you put them into combinations with your coach or partner holding focus pads or a kicking shield. Then you work them on a heavy bag. Then you integrate the techniques into sparring with an opponent.

Remember—take care of the legalities and licensing. Know the rules under which you're fighting. Practice all the permitted techniques. Keep working on your conditioning. Expect to go the distance. Fight hard and have a great time!

chapter eight

CHOOSING EQUIPMENT

When you choose equipment, the first thing you want to know is what kind your chosen type of kickboxing requires—whether you need foam-type equipment, cloth-elastic, instep shin-guard protectors, and types of gloves (such as regular boxing gloves or bare knuckle).

It's best to train with high-quality equipment, but this is not absolutely necessary. Nevertheless, make sure that any equipment you hit, or hit

gloves for training have more padding than you'd use when fighting. The heavier the glove the more padding it has.

with, is durable and strong. You'll pay the price for this kind of gear, but if you want to get involved and not just dabble in the sport, use equipment that will last when it takes a beating.

Gloves

You need three pairs of gloves: 10-ounce to 12-ounce leather gloves for fighting, depending on the weight class of the fighters, 4-ounce gloves for light bag work for speed drills, and 14-ounce to 16-ounce gloves for sparring. Either laced or velcro-closure gloves are fine, and buy gloves with thumb protectors.

The heavier the glove, the more padding it has. For training, use gloves with more padding than you'd use when fighting. For sparring, you need 16-ounce gloves if you weigh over 180 pounds. If you weigh 150 to 180 pounds, get 14-ounce gloves for sparring. If you weigh under 150 pounds, you need 12-ounce gloves for sparring. These weights and glove sizes apply to men and women.

Light, 4-ounce gloves are great for working speed drills on a light bag. This work is also beneficial to prepare for fighting a fast opponent, a "mover." Make sure that your light gloves have at least a half-inch of padding to protect your knuckles.

To compete as an amateur, you fight with 12-ounce gloves if you weigh over 156 pounds. If you weigh under 156 pounds, you need 10-ounce gloves for fighting.

Headgear

This equipment must be approved and is required at the amateur level. Headgear requirements for amateur kickboxing are the same as in amateur boxing, not in martial-arts point fighting.

Headgear for kickboxing offers protection for the jaw, chin, and back of the head. Fitting this equipment is important, because a great variety of adjustable headgear is now available. In addition to fit, be sure the headgear does not restrict your vision so much that you can't see where you're punching and kicking. For training purposes, you could use headgear with bars.

Leather headgear is better than foam. When foam headgear gets sweaty, it slides out of place.

headgear for kickboxing offers protection for the jaw, chin, and back of the head. Fitting this equipment is important, because a great variety of adjustable headgear is now available.

Foot and Shin Pads

Most of the time, Western-style full-contact kickboxing requires foot and shin guards, available from a variety of manufacturers. There is an enormous variety of shin guards on the market. Finding a comfortable pair is the key, and make sure the pair you buy covers your toes. You need to protect the toes from being broken on your partner's elbows. You might want to remove the laces that some foot pads have and sew in a leather bottom, at least for the balls of the feet. The leather helps you grip the canvas better. If the leather

Kickboxing usually requires foot and shin guards. Finding a comfortable pair is the key. Make sure the pair you buy covers your toes to protect them from being broken on your partner's elbows.

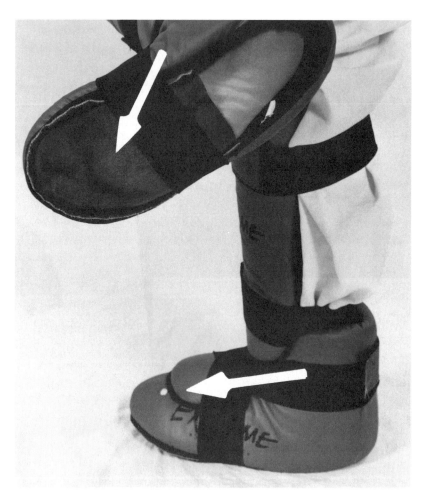

You might want to remove the laces that some foot pads have and sew in a leather bottom (top arrow), at least for the balls of the feet. The leather helps you grip the canvas better. If the leather becomes polished and smooth from wear, use a wire brush to scar the leather before a fight to restore its gripping power. The leather bottom also protects the foot better and keeps the pads better in place. You might also want to sew the shin guards to the top of the foot protector (bottom arrow). This helps keep both items in place.

becomes polished and smooth from wear, use a wire brush to scar the leather before a fight to restore its gripping power. The leather bottom also protects the foot better and keeps the pads better in place. You might also want to sew the shin guards to the top of the foot protector. This helps keep both items in place.

Foot gear and shin guards lined with felt are useful so that the guard doesn't slide on the foot when it becomes sweaty in several rounds of fighting. Dipped foam shin guards often slip when they become sweaty.

Speed Bag, In-between Bag

Using a speed bag helps you develop hand–eye coordination. A speed bag is used to practice punching, but it can be used for kicking. You should begin with a larger bag, and progress to a smaller one, which can be worked faster.

Because of the way it moves, an in-between bag is good for developing reaction time with kicks and punches. Most in-between bags are the same size. They are usually made with leather or vinyl on the outside, but leather on the

outside is more durable and lasts longer. Vinyl tears and cracks more easily. Adjust the bag's height—raise it for punches, drop it down for kicking. Most beginners use an in-between bag only for hand techniques.

Heavy Bags

A 70-pound cloth-filled heavy bag is best, if you can train with only one bag. Cloth-filled bags are harder than water-filled bags, which are often used in karate training. Water-filled bags cause less stress on the joints when punching and kicking, and less trauma; but they don't help you develop the same kind of power in kicks and punches as a regular heavy-duty heavy bag.

If you use only one bag, it's best not to use a canvas bag for kickboxing. Canvas is abrasive and can cut your skin. Canvas can also tear the outer materials on gloves and shin guards. Vinyl-covered bags are better because vinyl is durable and won't rip the outer coverings of bag gloves and shin guards.

Ideally you should train on three bags. A 165-pound water-filled bag is useful for working your power and to

simulate a fighter who doesn't move. You'll discover that a bag this heavy doesn't move a lot, either!

A 70-pound bag moves a little more. The 70-pound bag is good for all-around work and in the case where you have to choose only one bag.

If you use only one bag, it's best not to use a canvas bag for kickboxing. Canvas is abrasive and can cut your skin. Canvas can also tear the outer materials on gloves and shin guards. Vinyl-covered bags are better because vinyl is durable and won't rip the outer coverings of bag gloves and shin guards.

A 35-pound bag moves a lot—in fact, it flies all over the place! Work this lighter bag when you're training to fight someone who moves a lot. This light bag is very forgiving, so use it also when you're recovering from an injury, like bruised knuckles, or a muscle pull, for example.

Hand Wraps

Wrapping the hands adds support for the fingers and wrists. Learn how to wrap your own hands so you can do so without a trainer. Use self-working wraps with a loop for the fingers. This kind of wrap supports the wrists and fingers and offers less of a chance of injury.

Amateur kickboxing regulations on taping are specific. When you fight, you have to use surgical gauze and surgical tape—you can't use hand wraps in competition. Fighters are allowed only a certain amount of tape, and wrapped hands mustn't have bulges, gaps, or "padded" spots. The referee checking the tape does not want to see too much or too little tape. This check is performed by visual inspection,

there are many ways to wrap the hands. You should experiment to find the most comfortable wrap that supports your wrists, hands, and fingers. Large-handed people might want to wrap between each finger. Small-handed people may be more comfortable wrapping only between the pinkie and ring fingers and the thumb and index fingers, and circling the wrap around the knuckles.

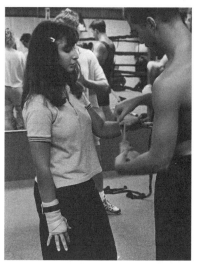

Wrapping the hands adds support for the fingers and wrists. Learn how to wrap your own hands so you can do so without a trainer. Use self-working wraps with a loop for the fingers. This kind of wrap supports the wrists and fingers and offers less of a chance of injury.

try this hand-wrapping method to start. First flex your fingers, pressing your palm outward and separating your fingers as much as possible. Catch the loop around your thumb.

begin winding the wrap in even turns up your arm as far as the gloves will reach. Then wind back to the wrist.

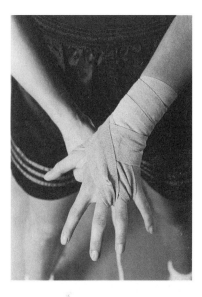

bring the wrap between each finger, starting between the pinkie and ring finger. Wrap once around the wrist each time you bring the tape between the fingers. Place the wrap between the fingers from the knuckles (top of the hand) to the palm, and then around the wrist.

after you bring the tape between the index and middle fingers, wrap around the wrist in the opposite direction. Then bring the wrap between the thumb and index finger.

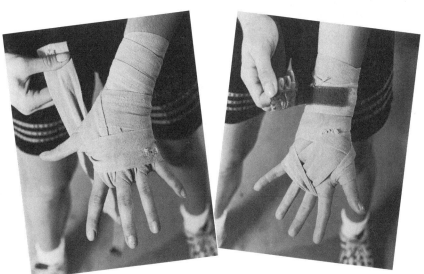

after you wrap between the thumb and index finger, finish by pressing the Velcro end in place.

often as you wrap the tape, and then each taped hand is sometimes initialed to show it's been checked. Referees must be certified by the sanctioning organization to evaluate and initial taped hands.

Wraps are also an important item of hygiene. They absorb the sweat inside your gloves, instead of the glove absorbing it. It's much easier to wash the wraps than to wash your gloves!

Some wraps are color-coded according to length. Wraps range from about 120 inches to about 180. Buy the longest wraps you need. If you have large hands, buy longer wraps. If you have small hands, buy shorter wraps.

There are many ways to wrap the hands. You should experiment to find the most comfortable wrap that supports your wrists, hands, and fingers. Large-handed people might want to wrap between each finger. Small-handed people may be more comfortable wrapping only between the pinkie and ring fingers and the thumb and index fingers, and circling the wrap around the knuckles.

Try this method to start: First flex your fingers, pressing your palm outward and separating your fingers as much as possible. Catch the loop around your thumb, and begin winding the wrap in even turns up your arm as far as the gloves will reach. Then wind back to the wrist. Bring the wrap between each finger, starting between the pinkie and ring finger. Wrap once around the wrist each time you bring the tape between the fingers. Place the wrap between the fingers from the knuckles (top of the hand) to the palm, and then around the wrist. After you bring the tape between the index and middle fingers, wrap around the wrist in the opposite direction. Then bring the wrap between the thumb and index finger. After you wrap between the thumb and index finger, finish by pressing the Velcro end in place.

However you decide to wrap your hands, let the feeling of wraps around your fingers and wrists, and gloves on your hands, be an invitation and a reminder to use these weapons.

the largest kicking shields benefit your trainer or coach, even though they work just fine for you. You might not be the trainer's or coach's only student, so he needs a lot of protection from the day-long onslaught of students battering him with kicks!

Focus Pads

Your coach or trainer must know how to use pads. Gloved focus pads are ideal. They feature a hard, flat striking surface with a glove-like leather back and an adjustable hand strap. You have a good, solid hit when you train with gloved focus pads. Rounded focus pads may cause you to slide off the target when you hit it. Some trainers prefer focus pads to Thai pads (described below, on page 92) because they force the fighter to focus on a smaller target, thus increasing accuracy.

Learning to hit a small target accurately is important. You have only about a two-inch target between your opponent's well-guarded torso and the bottom of his elbows. If you hit the floating ribs consistently, you'll hurt the opponent. Strike inaccurately on his guarded areas, and you'll cause little damage.

Kicking Shields

Vinyl-covered kicking shields are about two feet or slightly longer, eight to 12 inches thick, and 12 to 19 inches wide. Sewn-in forearm handles on the back let your coach or training partner hold on and move around as you kick. Air-filled shields are common in martial-arts training, but for kickboxing the more durable foam-filled shields are better.

The largest kicking shields benefit your trainer or coach, even though they work just fine for you. You might not be the trainer's or coach's only student, so he needs a lot of protection from the day-long onslaught of students battering him with kicks!

Mirrors

Using a mirror in the training area is not a necessity, but it helps you develop proper technique. A technique may feel right to you, but with a mirror you can see whether it is right. Your instructor or trainer can help you correct a technique using the mirror.

Shadow boxing in a mirror is good for developing movement, timing, and combinations, and to warm up and cool down.

Using a mirror in the training area is not a necessity, but it helps you develop proper technique. A technique may feel right to you, but with a mirror you can see whether it is right. Your instructor or trainer can help you correct a technique using the mirror.

INSTRUCTORS, TRAINERS, GYMS

Look for an instructor or trainer who knows kickboxing and who has contacts so that when you're ready, he can set up some fights for you. Some trainers can train you, but they don't have the contacts to help you start an amateur career. Call a variety of schools or go to matches and find out who the successful trainers are.

Observe the instructors and trainers. Are they out of shape, and do they smoke, or do they practice what they preach? Call your state athletic commission to learn which gyms are licensed and who the licensed promoters are. There are many traditional karate instructors who will tell you they'll teach you kickboxing, and they might be able to do that, but you need to ensure that they can, in fact, do that.

Pick a gym with a good ring and all the adequate training gear. If you have to bring your own stuff, that gym probably doesn't invest much in kickboxing. If you're going to a gym to learn how

Look for an instructor or trainer who knows kickboxing and who has contacts so that when you're ready, he can set up some fights for you. Some trainers can train you, but they don't have the contacts to help you start an amateur career. Call a variety of schools or go to matches and find out who the successful trainers are.

to kickbox, you want to look at whoever's running the place and their background, and consider if they have all the equipment to train you properly. The ring is important. You don't absolutely have to have one, but it helps. You could hook up ropes and learn some ring skills. Whether or not you train with a ring depends on how serious you are. A gym that is equipped with a good-quality ring is one that considers kickboxing a main sport, not a secondary activity.

Observe classes, and talk to those involved. See how many fights they've had, and how often fights become available. Consider price, and ask for rec-ommendations. This is comparative shopping. The most expensive facility might not be the best.

Through observation, get a good feel for those you're going to train with and for those who are going to train you. You're going to work often with partners. You can't always pick your training partners. If a lot of people are fooling around, if you observe a lot of unsafe activity, people doing whatever they want and not a lot of correction by instructors taking place, there is a greater chance of injury. Observe the quality of the instruction. By picking the gym, you're picking the people you want to train with.

Whether or not you train with a ring depends on how serious you are. A gym with a good-quality ring is one that considers kickboxing a main sport, not a secondary activity.

Thai Pads

Thai pads can be strapped to your partner's or coach's arms. These pads are useful for working roundhouse kicks. Your partner or coach can also strap a similar pad to the midsection so that you can use front kicks safely in combination with roundhouse kicks. Thai pads are smaller than kicking shields, so whoever holds the pads can move the arms more freely and move around the training area without losing control of the pads.

Groin Cup

This item of equipment is a standard boxing cup, but it's called a "tuck-under" because of the addition of kicking. A baseball cup, for instance, is flat, and is designed to protect the wearer from a straight-on shot. Tuck-under cups tuck under the body a little to protect against kicks coming from underneath.

Tuck-under cups are specially designed cups and are fitted by waist size. Some boxing types of men's groin protection are designed to be worn over the shorts.

Women should buy special chest protectors and groin protectors. To fit the chest protector correctly and comfortably, women might want to apply tape to the top edge.

Mouthpiece

Your mouthpiece has to fit right or it might affect your breathing. You might be used to a double mouthpiece if you come from a martial-arts back-

Thai pads can be strapped to your partner's or coach's arms. These pads are useful for working on roundhouse kicks. Thai pads are smaller than kicking shields, so whoever holds the pads can move the arms more freely and move around the training area without losing control of the pads.

ground, but a single mouthpiece with a double mold is better for kickboxing. This mouthpiece has a deep groove for the top teeth, into which you pour a shapable compound that hardens slightly and conforms to the top teeth. It also lets you form an impression of the bottom teeth in the mouthpiece's bottom. These mouthpieces also "stick" to the top teeth by suction when you open your mouth to breathe. You can cut away a little of the mouthpiece material in the back to prevent the gag reflex. Double mouthpieces with holes in the middle are ineffective for kickboxers.

Always train with your mouthpiece in, to get used to it. It will affect your breathing until you get used to it. In fact, it's important to use in training all the equipment you're going to fight with.

a medicine ball is the most vital conditioning aid. It is useful for abdominal training. Medicine balls are available in different weights. Make sure the one you get is a weight that you can at least lift.

Conditioning Aids

A medicine ball is the most vital item. It is useful for abdominal training (see Chapter 2). Medicine balls are available in different weights. Make sure the one you get is a weight that you can at least lift.

SELECTED SOURCES OF EQUIPMENT

■■■■■■■■■■■■■■■■■■■■■■■■■■■■■■■■■■■■■■■

Many companies sell kickboxing training equipment. Get catalogs from the following companies and see what's available. Your trainer or coach should also be able to equip you. Remember that the equipment you buy, train with, and ultimately fight with should match the rules of your kind of kickboxing.

Asian World of Martial Arts
11601 Caroline Road
Philadelphia, PA 19154-2177
1-800-345-2962
http://www.awma.com

Kwon, Inc.
3755 Broadmoor, S.E.
Grand Rapids, MI 49512
1-800-596-6872

Ringside, Inc.
9650 Dice Lane
Lenexa, KS 66215
913-888-1719
http://www.ringsideboxing.com

Century Martial Art Supply, Inc.
1705 National Blvd.
Midwest City, OK 73110-7942
1-800-626-2787
http://www.centuryma.com

Musashi International
1842 S. Grand Avenue
Santa Ana, CA 92705
1-800-982-2555

Index

LOUGHBOROUGH COLLEGE LIBRARY